AN ILLUSTRATED GUIDE TO

# American Freight Train Equipment

**Detailed Coverage of Box Cars, Refrigerator Cars, Covered Hopper Cars, Open Top Hopper Cars, Ore Cars, Flat Cars, Tank Cars, Intermodal Cars, Auto Racks, and Cabooses.**

## Patrick C. Dorin

D1073206

**Enthusiast Books**

1830A Hanley Road
Hudson, Wisconsin 54016 USA

## www.enthusiastbooks.com

Enthusiast Books are offered at a discount when sold in quantity for promotional use. Businesses or organizations seeking details should write to the Marketing Department, Enthusiast Books, at the above address.

Library of Congress Control Number: 2013916488

ISBN-13: 978-1-58388-306-8
ISBN-10: 1-58388-306-1

First printing, September 2013.

Printed in The United States of America

# TABLE OF CONTENTS

# ACKNOWLEDGMENTS

I have been very lucky to have the following folks who provided assistance with research and with a wide variety of photos for this book on freight car equipment: Harold K. Vollrath, Dan Mackey, Bob Blomquist, Bruce Black, Tim Schandel and others with the Lake Superior Railroad Museum in Duluth, Wally Ruce, Charles Wickman, and the Soo Line Historical Society. I also wish to thank Dylan Frautschi and the staff at Enthusiast Books for the editing work and layout of the book. Should anyone's name has been inadvertently missed, we trust it will be at the appropriate location within the book.

Without the time and kind assistance of these folks, the book would not have been possible. Thank you for your time, kind assistance and wisdom.

# INTRODUCTION

The purpose of this book on railroad freight cars is to illustrate and describe the different types of equipment operated in North America. Each type of freight car, such as box cars, is capable of handling multiple types of commodities.

Box cars, for example, are designed to handle commodities that need to be kept safe from the weather and other types of problems. Paper is just one example of the type of freight that is handled best in box cars. Another example of a box car commodity is auto parts. In order to handle the different types of commodities that require safe handling and weather protection, box car designs vary from only 40 feet in length to large cubic capacity 85-foot equipment.

The book covers the wide variety of equipment for each type of car. Equipment designs are based on the type of commodity that would be shipped. For example, 24-foot ore cars are designed to handle 75 to 85 tons of iron ore. High cubic capacity covered hopper cars are designed for handling grain traffic, while lower cubic capacity is designed for handling heavy commodities, such as cement.

Each chapter also illustrates the variety of color schemes and lettering for the different railroad equipment. The book covers equipment from the wide variety of railroads serving North America.

Best Wishes and Happy Railroading,

Patrick C. Dorin
Superior, Wisconsin
2013

# Chapter 1
# BOX CARS

The box car is basically a large box with side doors for loading and unloading freight shipments. The cars, currently in operation, range in size from 40 feet to 85 feet in length. The cars are designed to handle a wide variety of commodities, which can be packaged (such as smaller types of tools) or larger pieces of equipment.

Over the many years, thousands of commodities have been shipped in box cars. One example was grain. For many decades, when the harvest season began, empty box cars were assembled into trains out of Chicago, St. Paul, St. Louis and many other terminals and sent west to the Great Plains where much of North America's wheat and other grains were grown.

When the box cars were loaded with grain, an inside barrier sometimes known as a grain door was inserted into the car at the sliding outside door. The grain door was a few feet shorter than the height of the car. With this type of a system, the grain eleva-tors could load the car through the upper section of the opening. When the cars were unloaded at a flour mill or other destinations, the inside grain door was removed to permit an easier flow from the car. During the 1960s and '70s, new developments such as the 100-ton capacity covered hoppers replaced the box cars for grain traffic.

Moving well into the 21st Century, box cars are still a very important type of equipment for handling many types of cargo. There have been many innovations modifying the box cars, which includes damage-free equipment within the car to keep commodities from bouncing around during slack action of the train or other factors. Many box cars are equipped with cushion draw bars (part of the coupler system), which ease the stress on the box car loads.

The following photos and diagrams illustrate the wide variety of equipment that have been or are in service from the days of wood box cars to modern cars designed for such delicate freight as auto parts.

This DM&IR wood box car has weathered and the car numbers are not visible. The car is 40-feet long with outside bracing. This wood car has steel ends as well as steel doors. The car is a good example of equipment built in the early 1900s, and is now on display at the Lake Superior Railroad Museum in Duluth, Minnesota. *February 2013, Patrick C. Dorin*

Duluth, Missabe & Iron Range Railway wood box car, number 5132, is approximately 40 feet long and has a 30-ton capacity. The car was rebuilt in May 1965 at the Proctor, Minnesota, shops. This car is one of the few (if any others) survivors and is currently part of the Lake Superior Railroad Museum (LSRM) displays in Duluth, Minnesota. The car was painted in the darker box car red colors with white lettering. The car is shown here at the LSRM museum. Note the wood DM&IR caboose to the right. *Patrick C. Dorin*

Stock cars are not exactly what one would call a box car, but it does have similar designs with the sides built in such a way for the animals to be able to breath while en route to the stock yards. Northern Pacific car number 83099 is part of the display of freight equipment at the LSRM at Duluth. *Patrick C. Dorin*

Grand Trunk Western box car number 599975 is 58 feet long with a 77-ton capacity. This group was equipped with cushion drawbars to alleviate slack action effect on the cargo. Note the wording below the track and the GT—the Good Track Road. The Grand Trunk Western did a remarkable job in keeping the track at the best quality. The 599975's portrait was taken in Valparaiso, Indiana, in August 1989. *Patrick C. Dorin*

Burlington Northern rib side box car number 249097 was over 50 feet long. The car was painted in the BN's Cascade Green with white lettering. *Dan Mackey*

BN number 244890 was equipped with a plug door and cushion drawbars. The capacity of the car is slightly over 75 tons. *Dan Mackey*

Wisconsin Central box car number 25707, with cushion drawbars, is an example of the lettering during the WC's early years in the 1980s. The company purchased quite a few cars from other railroads to enhance its fleet to serve the increasing number of shippers and carloads. Notice the areas painted out in order to paint on the new reporting marks and car number. *Bob Blomquist*

The new Wisconsin Central began purchasing new box cars, such as the 26608 with side ribs and a plug door. The cars were painted in an attractive maroon color with yellow lettering, and white reporting marks. *Author's Collection*

WC number 20259 had quite a bit of graffiti, which has been painted out on this rib side modern box car. This car has a 95-ton capacity. *Author's Collection*

WC 20444 has the company's attractive color scheme of a bright maroon and gold lettering. *Bob Blomquist*

When the Soo's Wisconsin and Michigan lines were purchased by the new Wisconsin Central, many of the cars secured from other railroads simply received the WC reporting marks and numbers to begin with. The WC 16004 is in woodchip service. *Bob Blomquist*

A former Soo Line box car with rib sides and plug door has retained its original Soo lettering and its number, 18004, but has received WC reporting marks. *Bob Blomquist*

This rib side plug door box car, WC 20326, was repainted and received the new lettering illustrating the Wisconsin Central insignia as well as the full words, "Wisconsin Central." *Author's Collection*

Soo Line's 40-foot, single door box car number 45382 illustrates the new lettering that replaced the Soo's original insignia. It was very easy to see the enlarged SOO LINE lettering. This photo was taken in October 1987. *Author's Collection*

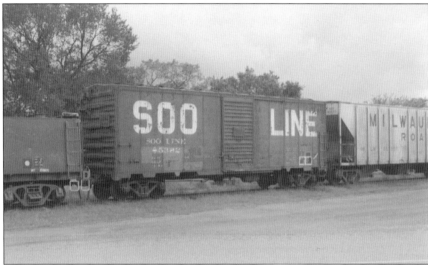

The Burlington Northern merger adopted an interesting insignia with a large B and the letter N enclosed within the B. BN number 249097 is a 50-foot rib side car with a large door designed for loading larger size shipments. This BN car was photographed in the Superior yard in May 1994. *Dan Mackey*

BN 286151 is a larger cubic volume, rib side, plug door box car. Paper is one type of commodity handled in this type of equipment. The car is cable of handling loads of just over 94 tons. The color scheme for this car is the BN's Cascade Green with the white lettering. *Dan Mackey*

Wisconsin Central 50-foot, rib side box car is, as one can observe, a former Minneapolis, Northfield and Southern Railway car. The car is equipped with cushion drawbars for the coupler system. The car's blue color with the red lettering is fading away. The blue colors with red lettering was a typical paint scheme for many of the MN&S box cars. *Dan Mackey*

This Great Northern hi-cube box car, number 138585, was repainted in the GN's new blue colors with white lettering, including the new "Goat" insignia without the Great Northern lettering. Note, however, that the GN did have the full name of the railroad in the upper left hand corner of the car. This double plug door car has a capacity of just over 73 tons. The car was photographed in Superior in September 1992, over twenty years since the Burlington Northern merger. *Dan Mackey*

Southern Pacific rib side, double door, box car number 247151 was equipped with a cushion under frame for absorbing slack action. The car was photographed in February 1993 at Superior, and was waiting to be switched to a paper mill for paper traffic. *Dan Mackey*

Great Northern 319463 was a hi-cube, plug door, rib side box car for paper traffic as well as other types of commodities. The car was also equipped with a cushion under frame, and was painted in the new blue GN colors with the new "goat" insignia without lettering. There was some talk, or at least a rumor, that the new modified GN insignia would be the insignia for the Burlington Northern merger. This car was photographed in Superior in April 1993, but had been painted in the mid-1960s. *Dan Mackey*

Wisconsin Central Double Plug Door car number 1117 was equipped with a cushion under frame and was operated for paper traffic and other commodities. The car had recently been modified as one can observe with the repainted areas on the doors and behind the crab irons at the right end of the car. This portrait was taken in Superior in August 1993. *Dan Mackey*

The Rail Box insignia stood for the company that provided equipment for the railroad companies to borrow for shipments. The lettering and the insignia on the right end of the car advertised, "The nationwide boxcar pool" plus the wording, "next load . . . any road." This particular car had been sold to the Southern Pacific and carries the SP reporting marks, plus it retained the car number for Rail Box. *Dan Mackey*

This rib side plug door box car, WC number 17266, was a former Soo Line box car that had been sold to the new Wisconsin Central. The car has a capacity of 77 tons. *Dan Mackey*

This Wisconsin Central rib side plug door box car, number 20459, is a prime example of how this new railroad company did eventually repaint and re-letter equipment purchased from other railroads, such as the Soo Line. This 50-foot car has a capacity of over 77 tons and its portrait was taken in September 1992. *Dan Mackey*

Western Pacific 50-foot plus double door box car, number 38252, had been repainted and received WP's final "Feather" insignia. The car's capacity was just over 73 tons. The paint scheme included yellow doors for this type of box car. *Dan Mackey*

Burlington Northern rib side double door box car number 222557 was painted the BN's Cascade Green color scheme, which caught many shipper's attention. This car was photographed in August 1993, and was operated for paper traffic as well as other types of high quality commodities. *Dan Mackey*

Bangor and Aroostook Railroad rib side box car number 5687 is from the State of Maine. It is another example of a 77-ton capacity car operated for high quality commodities. *Dan Mackey*

The Minnesota, Dakota and Western is a short line railroad in northern Minnesota. Its primary commodity traffic is paper as the railroad provides switching and other services for the mills. This 50-foot rib side car is equipped with a cushion under frame; note the words "Cushion Service" in the upper right hand corner of the car. *Dan Mackey*

Kansas City Southern Railroad box car number 749368 has a capacity of 159,600 pounds, or 79.8 tons. The KCS reporting marks and the car number are designed for catching peoples' attention to the KCS. *Dan Mackey*

The ICG reporting marks for this rib side box car, number 501866, stand for the wording, Illinois Central Gulf. This was the new name for the merger of the Illinois Central and the Gulf, Mobile and Ohio railroads. *Dan Mackey*

Kansas City Southern rib side box car, number 752061, has a 77-ton capacity. The car is painted a lighter brown than the typical box car red colors. *Dan Mackey*

Here is an example of a rib side box car from the Missouri Pacific Railroad, which had been merged into the Union Pacific. The car carries the MP reporting marks plus the Union Pacific insignia. *Dan Mackey*

Canadian National double door (plug door and regular sliding door) number 557115 was painted in a green color with the CN insignia over a map of North America. The insignia was designed to show that the CN was not simply a Canadian railroad, but included the United States. The Wisconsin Central and the Illinois Central railroads are part of the CN. *Dan Mackey*

This Minnesota, Dakota and Western box car number 8166 is part of a BN freight consist traveling south by the University station sign in the Twin Cities. The University of Minnesota in Minneapolis is located directly south of this location, and hence the station name. The MDW rib side box car is most likely loaded with paper from one the mills near International Falls, Minnesota. *Dan Mackey*

This CP Rail rib side, double plug door box car, carries the reporting marks for the Milwaukee Road. The Milwaukee Road was merged into the Soo Line, and later the Canadian Pacific exhibited more control over the Soo, which is one of the reasons why this CP Rail box car carries the MILW reporting marks. *Bob Blomquist*

The Bangor and Aroostook Railroad's reporting marks are "BAR." BAR number 8902 is basically a 50-foot car with a larger door. Note the short ladder or hand rail on each end of the car. The car is designed to handle paper traffic. *Dan Mackey*

This Detroit, Toledo and Ironton 80-foot plus, double plug door box car is designed for handling auto-parts for the automobile industry. DTI car number 25906 is handling parts for the Ford plant located in the Twin Cities area. The car is painted green with orange lettering. *Dan Mackey*

This Kansas City Southern 50-foot, plug door, rib side box car, number 170201, is painted a lighter brown with white lettering and numbers. The car is shown here in the Twin Cities (Minnesota) area in February 1993. Note the snow on the ground, which is typical in Minnesota from November until April. *Dan Mackey*

MSDR 194738 is painted a bright red with white lettering. This rib side car is also equipped with a cushion under frame. *Dan Mackey*

Northern Pacific plug door box car number 97760 is painted a darker green with white lettering for advertising the company's primary passenger train. To the right of the plug door are the words, "Scenic Route of the Vista Dome North Coast Limited." The car is also equipped with a cushion under frame. *Dan Mackey*

BCRAIL is the insignia for the British Columbia Railroad. This fifty-foot plus rib side box car carries the reporting marks BCOL, and car number 48005. This rib side, double door car is painted a dark green with white lettering. *Dan Mackey*

Southern Pacific 85-foot box car number 615256 has two sets of double plug doors on each side of the car. The car displays the wording HY CUBE (meaning a very large cubic area) on one set of doors, while the other set displays the words, HYDRA–CUSHION, which means cushion under frame for the couple system. The car was pretty well weathered when its portrait was taken. *Dan Mackey*

This Chicago and North Western double door box car, number 153154, is equipped with a cushion under frame and carries the insignia "Employee Owned." This insignia came about when the C&NW underwent a substantial amount of reorganizing after a number of disastrous years with financial difficulties. The car was photographed in January 1995; and as one can observe, it has some weathering showing up on both sides. *Dan Mackey*

This Burlington Route single door, 50-foot car has also taken on a substantial amount of weathering. The car number, 23271, is barely visible. *Dan Mackey*

This Minnesota Northern Railroad rib side, double door box car was designed for paper traffic as well as handling other commodities. The car is painted a darker green with white lettering and numbers. The car's portrait was taken in February 1994; and it is interesting that there is no snow on the ground. *Dan Mackey*

Prior to the Burlington Northern merger, the Great Northern adopted a new paint scheme, known as "The Big Sky Blue." GN 40-foot box number 20490 shows the size of the new simplified Great Northern insignia without the words "Great Northern." There was a thought of having the new BN color scheme as blue, however the color of choice was green. This car was photographed in Superior, Wisconsin, about 8 years after the merger in September 1978. *Bob Blomquist*

Over the many years since the BN merger, many of the freight cars in service on the Northern Pacific, the Great Northern and the Burlington Route retained their original reporting marks. This GN box car, number 5284, retained its GN reporting marks for the 15 years before it went to the scrap yard in 1986. Note that the numbers on the 40-foot box have been lined out. *Bob Blomquist*

The St. Louis–San Francisco Railroad was eventually absorbed into the Burlington Northern. The SL-SF 50-foot double door box car, number 155002, retained its original reporting marks as well as the company slogan, "Ship it on the Frisco." After the merger into the BN, the Frisco freight cars operated virtually all over the BN system. This car was photographed in Superior, Wisconsin, in the late 1980s. *Bob Blomquist*

Milwaukee Road 40-foot box car number 8900 was equipped with a plug door plus was insulated. The car's interior had compartments for the safe handling of a variety of commodities. The 8900 was built in May 1956 and was painted in a box car red scheme with white lettering and numbers. *Milwaukee Road Photo*

The Marinette, Tomahawk and Western Railroad Company was a short line that served paper mills in central Wisconsin. The MTW number 4548 was basically a 50-foot car with outside braces and a wide door. The car was painted green with white lettering and red and white MT&W insignia. The car is shown here in Superior, Wisconsin, between two gondolas loaded with pulpwood destined for a paper mill. *February 1985, Bob Blomquist*

This 50-foot, double door including a plug door was Fort Worth and Denver Railroad's box car number 5009. The FW&D (as well as the Colorado Southern) were subsidiaries of the Burlington Route. Although the car carried the name Burlington in bold lettering as well as the Burlington Route insignia, the car's reporting marks were FW&D. The letters DF, to the right of the car number, indicate that it is designed for Damage Free shipping. The car is also equipped with a Cushion under frame for the coupler system, which avoids much of the slack action for safe handling of commodities. The car was painted with a bright red color and white lettering and numbers. *Bob Blomquist*

This Milwaukee Road box car number 3010 was equipped with a cushion under frame as well as a plug door. The car was used for paper traffic as well as a variety of many other commodities requiring safe handling. *Superior, Nov. 1987, Bob Blomquist*

This top down view of a Milwaukee Road outside braced box car with a very light yellow door displays the type of roof designs for such equipment. The car is part of the 56500 series box cars. *Bob Blomquist*

Milwaukee Road outside braced 50-foot box car, number 56661 (Series 56600 to 56699), is equipped with 10-foot door and basically (almost but not quite) a flat roof. *Bob Blomquist*

Forty-foot Minneapolis, Northfield and Southern box car number 1089 (1000 to 1099) was equipped with a 6-foot door, and painted box car red with white lettering. The car not only carried the company insignia with the full wording of the company name, but also the large and attractive white letters to the right of the door. The MN&S was a short line that operated south from Minneapolis to Northfield and Randolph, a distance 45.2 miles and 54.1 miles to Northfield and Randolph respectively. The short line served several industries, and interchanged carloads and empties with several Class I railroads in the Minneapolis area. *Bob Blomquist*

This Milwaukee Road outside braced 50-foot plus box car, number 3558, series 3500 to 3599, provided safe shipping for a variety of commodities. The car was also equipped with a cushion under frame. *Bob Blomquist*

This double door box car with the North Western's Employee Owned insignia, is a fifty-foot plus car with the reporting marks, CGW, meaning the Chicago Great Western. The car number is 909 and part of the 900 to 999 series. As one may be able to observe, this particular car once had a roof walk and ladders extending to the top of the car. Note that the ladders have been shortened, and the "catwalk" has been removed.

This Canadian Pacific 50-foot plus, plug door box car, was painted in a yellow scheme with black lettering and numbers. CP number 166563 (166549 to 166592 series) has lost quite a bit of the yellow color off the plug door. The car was built in March 1972 and the portrait was taken in April 2006. *Bob Blomquist*

Still another Canadian Pacific plug door box car, number 81029 (80967 to 81216 series) was painted in a green color scheme with the company name as CP Rail. *Bob Blomquist*

Here is an example of a 50-foot Soo Line box car, number 15560 (15500 to 15599), originally owned and operated by the Duluth, South Shore and Atlantic Railroad. One can barely see the original insignia to the left of the door, and the large DSS&A lettering to the right. The car just happens to be in grain service as one can observe the portable grain door inserted in the opening to keep the grain from pouring out the door. *Bob Blomquist*

The Duluth, Winnipeg and Pacific Railway owned and operated an excellent fleet of 50-foot plug door cars, such as number 403583, 403500 to 403749 series. The car was equipped with a cushion under frame, and handled a substantial amount of paper traffic. Note the DW&P reporting marks as DWC. The railroad was (and is) owned by the Canadian National, and it is believed that the "C" meant for Canadian service. *Bob Blomquist*

MSDR number 194738 is a 50-foot car with a 10-foot door, and is painted an attractive bright red color. The car is part of the Mississippi Delta Railroad fleet, series 194,000, which is headquartered at Clarksdale, Mississippi. The car's portrait was taken in September 1992. *Dan Mackey*

This view of WC 27202 has identical car ends as the WC 24044 previously illustrated. *Dan Mackey*

WC rib side box car number 24044, series 24000-24349, is a 58-foot car with a 10-foot door. The car is painted an attractive brighter maroon with a gold insignia and the words Wisconsin Central. The reporting marks and number is painted white. *Dan Mackey*

The Wisconsin Central purchased a fleet of cars from other railroads, and simply painted out the previous railroad's reporting marks and replaced them with WC and the new number. WC number 49765 was purchased from the former Minneapolis, Northfield and Southern. The car retained its original colors and lettering for quite some time after being purchased by the WC. *Dan Mackey*

Another example of a 40-foot box car from the Chicago and North Western Railroad, number 8449, had the complete name of the railroad and the CNW reporting marks, plus the large letters C&NW instead of the common North Western insignia. This car displays a substantial amount of weathering and the words and numbers no longer stand out. However, fortunately, they are still visible, especially the reporting marks "CNW" and the car number. *Dan Mackey*

Railroads often purchased box cars from other railroads. In this case, the car was purchased by the Missouri Pacific from the Lake Erie, Franklin and Clarion Railroad Company. Except for the new reporting marks "MP" and number 219, the car has retained its original owner's yellow color scheme along with the insignia. As one can observe, this is an outside braced steel car with a large door. *Dan Mackey*

This double door, outside braced steel box car, Southern Pacific Car number 217151, was painted in the box car red scheme with white lettering with exception of the yellow wording "CUSHION CAR." *Dan Mackey*

This Minnesota, Dakota and Western green box car, number 10077, was designed for handling paper traffic from northern Minnesota. *Dan Mackey*

This former Southern Pacific outside braced steel car was sold to a short line company, with the reporting marks, WCTR. The official name of the railroad is WCTU Railway Company and is headquartered in Atlanta, Georgia. This railroad operated 14 miles of road. Car number 243823 was purchased sometime in the first decade of the 21st Century.

WCTR number 101922 has an outside length of 58 feet, 3 inches. The door opening is 16 feet. *Dan Mackey*

This photo illustrates the type of latches that are used to secure the door tight when it is closed. *Dan Mackey*

It is not always easy to observe a roof on a box car. However, this North Louisiana and Gulf (reporting marks NLG) number 5291 had a silver roof with the body of the car painted green with white lettering. This car is in the fifty-foot category. *Dan Mackey*

# Chapter 2
# REFRIGERATOR CARS

Refrigerator cars were designed for the purpose of handling perishable food and other commodities in need of protection from the heat. Originally, refrigerator cars were designed with hatches at both ends of the roof for loading ice to keep the interior cold for the preservation of foods. For many years, the cars were of wood construction, and then later built with steel with the same type of design.

The requirement for the ice meant that the cars had to be spotted at ice loading facilities. The cars were always loaded with ice prior to the loading of the perishable foods, such as fruits, vegetables, and meat. Once the cars were loaded, they were either handled in solid trains for refers, or were part of blocks of cars destined for specific destinations. One example of refer train services was the handling of fruit grown in the western states that were en route to destinations in the Midwest and through to the East Coast.

The Great Northern handled solid trains of apples during the harvest season. While en route, the trains would need to be spotted at a location for new loads of ice in order to preserve the fruit. The same was true with trains on the Illinois Central handling bananas from the Gulf Coast.

During the 1940s, there were new designs on the drawing boards for refrigerator cars. The new cars were known as "mechanical refers" and did not require ice.

Many folks may remember the days when homes were equipped with ice boxes for the food. They were kept cold with the service from ice companies that delivered ice by truck to the homes. Electric refrigerators were soon available that eliminated the need for large blocks of ice.

The same happened in the railroad industry with the new mechanical refers. No longer did the cars have to be set out for ice along the route. With the new equipment, perishable fruits, vegetables, and meat could be delivered much quicker, and with improved quality.

The cars that required ice were generally in the 40-foot category. The new mechanical cars came in the 50-foot length and up to 60 feet.

Refrigerator cars were either owned by the railroad, or were owned by railroad subsidiary or a private company. If owned by the railroad itself, the reporting marks were of the railroad. If owned by a subsidiary or by a private company, the reporting marks were of the company. For example, the Western Fruit Express was owned by the Great Northern Railway and carried the reporting marks WFEX. The Soo Line leased refrigerator cars from the Union Refrigerator Transit, and carried the reporting marks URTX. The Soo Line also owned equipment with the SOO reporting marks.

The following photos illustrate the variety of refers operated in North America.

Fruit Grower Express mechanical refer number 12160 is a 50-foot plus car with a plug door and cushion under frame. The car is painted a light yellow with insignias for the FGE and the words "Solid Cold" outlined in blue. The reporting marks of FGMR, the car number and the data are in black. *Dan Mackey*

This Burlington Northern mechanical refrigerator car has the reporting marks of BNFE (car number 19501). The FE means Fruit Express and the car is actually part of the Western Fruit Express. The wording for Western Fruit Express can be observed below the BN insignia to the right of the plug door. The car is painted white with black lettering. *Dan Mackey*

Here is an example of a much older wood refrigerator car owned and operated by the Duluth, South Shore and Atlantic Railroad. The car's reporting marks were DSS&A, and the car number 5067. Its portrait was taken in Marquette, Michigan, in April 1963, about 3 years since the DSS&A was merged into the Soo Line Railroad. The car has faded substantially, as one can barely see the reporting marks and the car number. The word "refrigerator" was near the top of the car just to the left of the ladder on the right side of the car. It is not sure, but there could have been a DSS&A insignia just below the word "refrigerator." *Bruce Black Photo, Collection*

In order to be equipped with ice, the non-mechanical refers need to be loaded with ice at terminals with high level loading areas. This icing platform is a bit higher than the cars that are to be loaded to the left of the platform. The ice hatches on top were opened, and then large blocks of ice slid into the compartments at the end of each car. This is one example of the type of loading facilities that were in operation on the railroads for decades. *Lake Superior Railroad Museum*

The refer in this photo is known as an "express refrigerator car," and was operated as part of the passenger train consists. This photo shows how the ice was loaded into ice compartments at each end of the car. Note the block of ice which is being moved into the opening to be loaded in the car for the preservation of food shipments. As one can observe to the right, it is obvious that this car is part of a passenger train. *Lake Superior Railroad Museum*

For many years, wood refrigerator cars were common on the North American Railroads. This Great Northern Railway subsidiary Western Fruit Express was still in operation in the late 1960s, and even into the 1970s. This car was painted in a yellow scheme with the WFEX number 73989 for its reporting marks and number. *Lake Superior Railroad Museum*

The wood cars were eventually replaced by steel cars, such as this Burlington Route refer with a photo including a group of officials to welcome a new ice car. The refrigerator car doors were designed to have a close fitting to keep the cold air from escaping the car. *Lake Superior Railroad Museum*

BREX, Burlington Route express car number 5000 illustrates the type of ends that were common for the steel refrigerator cars. *Lake Superior Railroad Museum*

This Burlington Route refer illustrates the type of plug doors that replaced the former hinged doors on the newer equipment starting in the 1960s. This is a Burlington Route publicity photo with four railroad officials for the purpose of illustrating the progress that the Burlington was making with its new equipment designed to better serve shippers. *Lake Superior Railroad Musuem*

The ultimate in refrigerator car design included "hydraulic cushioning." Note the extension of the coupler system at the right end of the car. The reporting marks for the Burlington Route refrigerator cars was BRCX for the subsidiary company, Burlington Refrigerator Express. This photo of BRCX number 5300 illustrates the new plug door system applied to the newer refrigerator car fleet on many railroads. Although difficult to see, it appears that this car was built in 1966. *Lake Superior Railroad Museum*

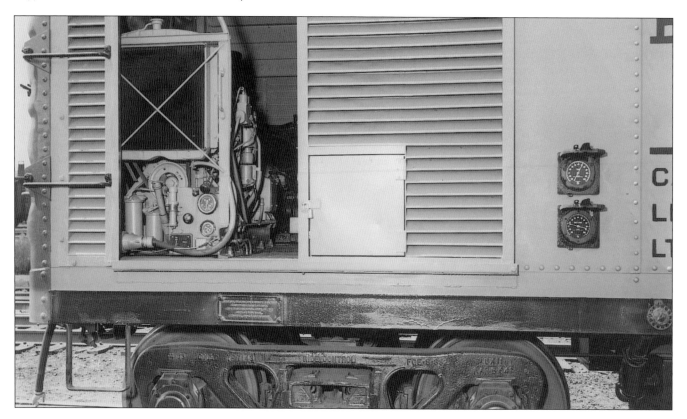

This view shows the interior of the compartment for the motor used for providing the refrigeration for the mechanical refers, as they were known. *Lake Superior Railroad Museum*

This photo shows a close up of the type of hinges used for the doors on the refrigerators cars. *Lake Superior Railroad Museum*

The Burlington Route also provided piggyback service for perishable commodities. Note the refrigeration unit just to the left of highway wheels. Burlington trailer number 6797 is a prime example of how intermodal service could benefit both the agricultural and the food market industries. *Lake Superior Railroad Museum*

# Chapter 3
# COVERED HOPPER CARS

The covered hopper car is designed for carrying bulk commodities with a need for protection from the environment. There are many types of commodities handled by covered hoppers, including cement, specific types of sand and grain just to name a few.

The covered hopper car is similar to an open type car but with a cover that is equipped with loading hatches. The hatches can be opened at a loading facility, and when the car is fully loaded, the hatches are closed. The car, or an entire unit train of grain, is picked up and handled to the destination. At that location, hopper doors at the bottom of the car are opened for the unloading process.

Smaller hopper cars are used for various types of commodities, such as cement, that need protection from the environment. Larger covered hopper cars are designed for commodities such as grain. Grain has a much lighter weight per cubic yard than commodities such as sands, cement and other loads.

There is a wide variety of covered hoppers on the railroads. Many have the hopper doors below the car, but there are also air slide covered hoppers. The latter cars are unloaded through a pipe system hooked up to the car at the destination, and it sucks the load out of the car.

The earlier covered hopper cars had a capacity ranging from 40 to 50 tons. This grew over the years to cars now designed to handle 100-ton loads.

Covered hopper cars are owned by railroad companies, as well as private companies. It all depends on the type of commodities shipped as well as the destination requirements for unloading.

The following photos illustrate the various types of covered hoppers in service in North America.

Here are two examples of the once very common 70-ton capacity covered hoppers. BN 424726 to the left has round roof hatches for loading, while the car to the right has square hatches. The car to the right has suffered a lot from the weather, and it is nearly impossible to see the reporting marks and the number series. However, it is former Northern Pacific car number 7578. These two cars illustrate the typical designs with the types of ribs and the exterior showing the slopes leading to the hoppers. *Robert Blomquist*

The Great Northern invested in a fleet of smaller 100-ton capacity hoppers for handling cement and other commodities. The GN 173988 was photographed in Superior, Wisconsin, in June 1993. *Bob Blomquist*

The Chicago and North Western covered hopper number 175571 was part of the consist of a C&NW transfer on the south side of St. Paul next to the Mississippi River. *Dan Mackey*

C&NW 175280 is another example of the newer 100-ton capacity covered hoppers for various types of high density commodities. The car's paint and lettering scheme was very attractive and drew the attention of many folks. *Dan Mackey*

Soo Line Air Slide covered hopper 69260 was unloaded by attaching a free flowing pipe system to unload the commodity. *Patrick C. Dorin Collection*

Burlington Northern Air Slide hopper 415354 was a 92-ton capacity car. With its box type design, this type of car had two hoppers for unloading. *Dan Mackey*

Soo Line covered hopper number 74981 was designed for grain traffic. Note the grain symbol toward the right end of the car. *Dan Mackey*

BNSF grain hopper number 495274 has just over 100-ton capacity. The equipment has worked out quite well for wheat and other grains grown throughout the Prairie States from Texas to the Canadian Border. The 495274 illustrates the new paint scheme and the BNSF's new insignia. This photo was taken in Superior, Wisconsin, an important Great Lakes port for shipping grain not only within North America, but to Europe and other continents as well. *Patrick C. Dorin, Summer 2012*

Covered hopper cars are not only owned by the railroad companies, but also by shippers. WLPX number 44637 is an example of a private car company. Notice the "X" as part of the reporting marks, which indicates private ownership. *Patrick C. Dorin*

Covered hopper car, BN 456351 is in the original Burlington Northern green color scheme with the large BN insignia. The car is shown here in Superior in grain service. *Patrick C. Dorin*

Here is an interesting design for a covered hopper. The sides of the car are rounded, similar to but not quite like a tank car. Canadian Pacific 388623 carries the CP Rail insignia, as shown here on the Soo Line Railroad in Superior. The car is in the 100-ton capacity category for grain service. *Patrick C. Dorin*

The Chicago and North Western was a major grain hauler. The company invested in 100-ton capacity cars such as the CNW 180468. The car was painted with what could be called an orange yellow scheme. The insignia is the Employee Owned design with the North Western wording and "Employee Owned" in the upper and lower parts of the circle. *Dan Mackey*

Another type of design for a covered hopper is shown with the BN 445015. The car is part of consist of a train just south of St. Paul. *Dan Mackey*

43

Great Northern covered hopper number 171522's lettering illustrates the type of traffic the car was built for. Note the words "Grain Loading" on the side. *Dan Mackey*

Burlington Northern covered hopper number 450234. This group of cars had a load capacity of 97.5 tons. *Dan Mackey*

This photo illustrates the type of roof hatches for loading grain into these types of grain haulers. Note the walkways on top of the car, which are designed for grain elevator staff to walk on top to open the hatches for loading. Note the green colors on the walkways (sometimes known as "catwalks") on the car to the left of BN 468638. *Dan Mackey*

BN covered hopper number 460896 is shown here in the green color scheme with various amounts of rust and weathering taking over. The car is in grain service at Superior, Wisconsin. *Dan Mackey*

Great Northern grain hopper number 171706 is a 100-ton capacity covered hopper for "Grain Loading," as illustrated with the lettering on the side of the car. This was the type of car that replaced box cars for the grain traffic. *Bob Blomquist*

Many companies, such as Pillsbury (reporting marks: PTLX), owned and operated 100-ton capacity covered hoppers for grain traffic. *Wally Ruce*

Great Northern grain car number 171406 was in an attractive color scheme of green with white lettering. It was designated as a grain car including the lettering "Grain Loading." The car was photographed in Kansas City as is evident with the barely visible lettering, "Kansas City Livestock Exchange" on the building in the background. *Dan Mackey*

C&NW number 179038 is another example of the 100-ton capacity grain cars in service for the Chicago and North Western. The insignia includes the working "Employee Owned" instead of the customary words "Chicago" in the upper circle and "System" in the lower part of the circle. *Dan Mackey*

When the C&O and B&O, and other regional railroads as well, merged, the new name for the company was the "Chessie System" as shown by the wording to the right end of the car. Note the large "C" with the cat resting inside, and the new reporting marks CSXT. The new color scheme was a yellow-orange with black lettering. *Dan Mackey*

Another example of a Chessie System covered hopper with the CSXT reporting marks with a light grey color scheme. *Dan Mackey*

Many of the 100-ton capacity grain covered hoppers on the Soo Line, such as SOO 74463, carried a grain of wheat as part of the décor. *Dan Mackey*

A top down view of the loading hatches on SOO 76534. *Dan Mackey*

Another example of a top down view of the loading hatches is this former Soo Line car, which has been sold to another company and as yet does not have new reporting marks or numbers. However, the car does illustrate the box car red or brown scheme used for this type of a grain car. *Dan Mackey*

Soo Line grain car with rib sides, car number 70149 is shown here in Superior, Wisconsin. *Dan Mackey*

Soo Line Air Slide covered hopper number 69225. *Dan Mackey*

The reporting marks for this 70-ton covered hopper are WC 69112. This car was purchased by the new Wisconsin Central from the Soo Line railroad as is obvious with the lettering. *Dan Mackey*

BNSF covered hopper number 495274 has a 112.5-ton capacity. The car has a very attractive paint scheme of a brighter box car red with the white lettering, including the BNSF insignia. The car has a capacity of 112.5 tons, and is shown here in grain service at Superior, Wisconsin, in September 2012. *Patrick C. Dorin*

# Chapter 4
# OPEN TOP HOPPER CARS

Open top hopper cars are designed for hauling shipments such as coal, sand, rocks, gravel and other material that can be easily loaded, and then emptied through the hopper doors at the bottom of the car.

There have been many designs over the past decades since the 1880s. At the beginning, such equipment was built with lumber. As steel became more prominent, and it was evident that steel would be useful for building railroad cars, hopper cars were a good design.

Since the 1920s steel hopper cars were designed at first for about 40-ton loads. It was not long into the 1940s and '50s that the capacities were growing from 50- to 75-ton capacities. It was not much

longer until 90-ton capacities were being designed and built for a variety of commodities. Approaching the 1990s the 100-ton capacity cars were hitting the rails. Each increase in capacity meant larger cars with more cubic space.

Moving into the 21st Century were equipment designs for handling 110 tons of coal or other bulk products. Furthermore, with the larger cubic capacity, aluminum began to be used for hopper car construction. Aluminum is less heavy than steel, and thus the capacity could be increased.

The focus of this chapter is to illustrate the variety of hopper cars over the decades and how they are operated.

Open top hopper cars are a very effective method for handling loads such as coal, stone, sand, ores and other types of bulk material that would not be affected by rain or snow. The cars are easily loaded and the bottom hopper doors can provide a relatively easy unloading process. There can be some difficult unloading if the commodity is affected by freezing cold weather. In such a situation, not only must the hopper be open, but the material may have to be punched out which can be difficult as well as dangerous. This photo illustrates a Wisconsin Central crew on the Lakefront in Ashland, Wisconsin, with two loaded coal hoppers from one of the coal docks. Coal for power plants is brought into Ashland by ship, and transferred to rail cars for movement to the destinations. *Dan Mackey*

This top down photo illustrates part of the interiors of the open top cars. Notice the two types of rock material in the cars to the right of the covered hoppers. This photo was taken at the former Great Northern yard (now BNSF) in Superior, Wisconsin. *Patrick C. Dorin*

Soo Line hopper number 60309 is a 100-ton capacity hopper with a partial load of coal, which is barely visible toward the bottom of the car. The photo was taken in Superior in October 1992. *Patrick C. Dorin*

Burlington Northern 528637 is a 100-ton capacity car in coal service. Although the car has hopper doors, the car is unloaded at a power plant with a rotary dumper. Although barely visible to the left of the car, the air hoses are on this side of the couplers. Again, barely visible in the white section at the right end of the car is the lettering, "Rotary Coupler End." This set of cars, part of a unit train, had just been unloaded at a coal dock for transferring the Montana coal to Great Lakes ships for movement to power plants in Marquette and Detroit, Michigan. *Patrick C. Dorin*

CSXT number 801044 is a 100-ton capacity car for handling coal loads. The CSXT is the new reporting mark regarding the merger of the Chessie System and the Seaboard System railroads. *Dan Mackey*

Northern Pacific number 87856 is a rock ballast car, which is used for spreading the rock foundation of the railroad track. This particular car has a capacity of over 75 tons and is an outside braced steel car. *Bob Blomquist*

Great Northern car number 70038 is a triple hopper car with a 77-ton capacity. *Dan Mackey*

Chessie System coal hopper number 192416 is a triple hopper car with the Chesapeake and Ohio reporting marks. The photo was taken during the summer of 1993. Chessie System equipment also included reporting marks for the Baltimore and Ohio and the Western Maryland. *Dan Mackey*

Chicago and Eastern Illinois Railroad hopper number 588345 was a 100-ton capacity car. The C&EI was part of the Missouri Pacific Railroad System, as one can observe with the MoPac insignia, which included the C&EI within the circle. This photo was taken in 1991 in the Chicago area. *Patrick C. Dorin*

C&O quad hopper coal car number 358480 had a 100-ton capacity. *Dan Mackey*

Chessie System triple coal hopper received new reporting CSXT with the merger with the Seaboard System. Car number 832259 is a 100-ton capacity car, and was photographed in a Wisconsin Central train in August 1993. *Dan Mackey*

This Chicago and North Western 100-ton hopper was eventually sold off to a private company with the reporting marks HLMX and a new car number of 43515. The car retained its green color scheme and the C&NW insignia for a while. The photo was taken in the Burlington Northern yard in Superior in the 1990s. *Patrick C. Dorin*

After the merger between the Burlington Northern and the Santa Fe, freight equipment received BNSF reporting marks and basically the former Santa Fe insignia with the words Burlington Northern Santa Fe. The BNSF number 646835 is in coal service at Superior, Wisconsin. *Patrick C. Dorin*

BNSF coal hopper number 645321 has the new BNSF insignia with the letters and the Wedge. *Patrick C. Dorin*

CNW hopper number 880039 has five hopper doors. Note the small insignia above the reporting marks. *Dan Mackey*

Algoma Central hopper number 8605 has just over a 100 tons capacity. The car was part of a Wisconsin Central train in Northwestern Wisconsin. *Dan Mackey*

CSXT hopper number 831915 has over a 100-ton capacity for coal haulage. The Chessie System freight equipment at one time carried the reporting marks of the different railroads such as the Chesapeake and Ohio (C&O) and Baltimore and Ohio (B&O). As time went on, the CSXT became the standard after the merger with the Seaboard System. *Dan Mackey*

The Wisconsin Central (now owned by the Canadian National) purchased a great deal of equipment from other railroads after it was incorporated in the mid 1980s. The Wisconsin and Michigan lines were sold off to the new WC after the Soo Line and the Milwaukee Road merged. WC 57537 was a former 100-ton capacity Clinchfield Railroad hopper car as one can see with the lettering. *Dan Mackey*

Great Northern ballast car number 78141 had a 77-ton capacity for rock ballast. The ballast cars not only served in work trains but also in revenue service for transporting various types of rock and stone material for road repair and construction. *Author's Collection*

Another example of a ballast car with the hopper doors providing both a center of track or outside the rail dumping. WC number 227 had just over a 100-ton capacity. *Dan Mackey*

Ballast car BN 957150 was a former Great Northern car. Photographed at Superior, Wisconsin, in September 1992.

Burlington Northern aluminum coal car number 533657 has a load limit of 219,300 pounds. *Author's Collection*

KCPL are the reporting marks for Kansas City Power. The car is part of a unit train owned by the Power Company. The car is equipped with four hopper doors. *Dan Mackey*

BN 575425 is a rotary dump flat bottom coal hauler, and serves in unit train service for coal haulage from Montana or Wyoming to the Midwest. *Patrick C. Dorin*

Burlington Route, CB&Q reporting marks, 50-ton capacity hopper is a typical example of the rib side 34- and 35-foot cars. The car was en route to a scrap yard as indicated by the car with a line painted through the reporting marks and the car number. *Superior, 1986, Bob Blomquist*

This 100-ton capacity coal hopper had been in unit train service for the Burlington Northern for several years. As the BN purchased newer equipment, many of the cars were sold to various regional railroads. In this case, the car number 33040 was sold to the Wisconsin Central Railroad, the spin off from the Soo Line–Milwaukee Road merger. The car is shown here at the BNSF yard at Superior. *Patrick C. Dorin*

Great Northern car number 70234 is listed with a capacity of 154,000 pounds, 77 tons. The car had not received new BN reporting marks or numbers for quite some time after the Burlington Northern merger. The car was painted with a lighter box car red color, and still carried the original Great Northern insignia in the upper left hand corner. *Dan Mackey*

Burlington Northern hopper car number 551517 is part of a coal train, and has not yet received BNSF reporting marks, as illustrated with the BNSF number 646835 to the right. The BN car has a capacity listed at 100 tons, while the car to the right has a slightly higher capacity in the neighborhood of 103-ton limit. *Superior, Patrick C. Dorin*

The Burlington Northern Santa Fe merger brought in the new reporting marks of BNSF. Car number 646835, part of a unit coal train consist at Superior, Wisconsin, has just gone through a rotary coal dumper for delivering coal to a coal dock for shipment by a Great Lakes vessel to an eastern Great Lakes area power plant, which in this shipment could be at Detroit, Michigan. The 646835 has the original BNSF insignia, which was a modification of the former Santa Fe insignia with the additional words, "Burlington Northern." *Patrick C. Dorin*

The BNSF later adopted an insignia with the letters "BNSF" with a line below the letters. The line below the letters is often called a wedge. This photo illustrates the change in the BNSF insignia history. *Superior, Patrick C. Dorin*

This 100-ton plus capacity coal hopper was sold by the Chicago and North Western (note the C&NW insignia) to a private car operator for coal operations. Note the reporting marks HLMX, and the new number 43515 applied to the car. The car was painted in the C&NW green with yellow lettering. *Patrick C. Dorin*

# Chapter 5
# ORE CARS

The primary transportation equipment for handling various types of ores are known as "ore cars." Most of the ore cars built and operated in North America were for the transportation of iron ore. There were and are many ore mines and pelletizing plants in Minnesota, Michigan and Ontario. There were several mines in northern Wisconsin, however, as of the late 20th Century, there are no longer any operating. However, there have been plans that have not yet been implemented for new mining activity in northern Wisconsin in the Mellen–Hurley area.

Virtually all of the ore cars that were or are now in operation in Michigan and Minnesota were 24 feet long, coupler to coupler length. The 24-foot design fit perfectly on the ore docks, which were built with 12-foot dumping pockets on top of the ore docks. Thus, a string of 24-foot ore cars would fit over every other pocket for unloading. The equipment had to be carefully spotted so that each car fit directly over the pocket for dumping. When one set of pockets were loaded to capacity for loading the ore boats, the next set of ore car movements covered the pockets that were not yet loaded.

The ore car history started with wooden ore cars of less than 30-ton capacity. The early steel ore cars were constructed with 50-ton capacities. This later developed into designs for 70- or 75-ton capacities. By the 1960s, there were some 24-foot ore cars designed with an 85-ton capacity.

Still later there were ore car designs for the Burlington Northern (later Burlington Northern Santa Fe)

that are 35 feet long and are unloaded through car dumpers rather than on the ore docks.

Moving into the second decade of the 21st Century, the vast majority of ore cars in Michigan and Minnesota are the 24-foot variety. The newest ore cars recently placed into operation were purchased by the Duluth, Missabe and Iron Range Railway, which is now owned by the Canadian National. The cars carry the DMIR reporting marks with the CN insignia.

It should be mentioned that a number of the pocket type of ore docks are still in operation. The former Chicago and North Western ore dock in Escanaba has been replaced by a low level dock, and the ore cars are unloaded through a dumper. The pellets are then stockpiled, and are transferred to the ore dock for boat loading with a conveyor system. The former Great Northern ore docks still stand, but are no longer operated (with the pellets being transferred to a silo dock with a conveyor belt system).

There are several hopper ore car types that are longer than 24 feet. One example is the LTV ore cars that were unloaded at Taconite Harbor on the North Shore of Lake Superior.

The North Shore Mining Company railroad operates flat bottom ore cars for the pellet plant at Silver Bay, Minnesota, on the North Shore.

The following diagrams and photos illustrate the types of ore cars in operation in the Lake Superior Region.

The Duluth, South Shore and Atlantic Railroad, the Soo Line and the Chicago and North Western Railroad were among the last railroads to operate 50-ton capacity ore cars in the Lake Superior region. The DSS&A was absorbed into the Soo Line around 1960. However, many of their 50-ton ore cars were still in operation through the 1960s. DSS&A 9061, a 50-ton car, is shown here at Marquette, Michigan, in 1965. *Patrick C. Dorin*

DSS&A 9609, a 50-ton capacity ore car, was among the last of this type of car, known as the Summers ore cars. This car was in service at Marquette in 1965. The Soo Line also owned a fleet of identical cars. *Patrick C. Dorin*

Still another type of 50-ton ore car in operation on both the Soo Line and the DSS&A was this group of slanted end cars. DSS&A 9659 is shown here at the Marquette, Michigan, ore yard, which served the ore dock in the downtown area. *Patrick C. Dorin*

This DSS&A 50-ton ore car is so rusted it is very difficult to determine the number of the car. It appears to be 9091, but this may not be correct. *Patrick C. Dorin*

The C&NW had a sizeable group of 50-ton ore cars built in the 1920s. C&NW 120593 was built in June 1923, and operated in ore service for both the Gogebic and Menominee Iron Ranges in northern Michigan. This group of ore cars was rebuilt in 1957-'58 and painted a box car red scheme with white lettering including the C&NW insignia. *Patrick C. Dorin*

The C&NW also operated a fleet of 70-ton capacity ore cars, later listed with a 77-ton capacity when rebuilt in 1965. The 70-ton cars were first operated only between the Menominee Range and Escanaba, Michigan; later into the late 1950s they also served the Gogebic Range with the ore moving to Ashland, Wisconsin. This was feasible when the C&NW began operating over the Soo Line concrete ore dock instead of C&NW's number 3 timber ore dock. The Soo Line dock had more room between tracks. *Charles R. Wickman*

The Milwaukee Road also operated a fleet of 70-ton ore cars, and were later rebuilt with extensions for handling iron ore pellets in northern Michigan. Milwaukee Road 76794 is shown here with a capacity of 154,000 pounds. The HO gauge Round House rectangular side model ore cars were based on the Milwaukee Road design, which was different from the ore cars with a similar capacity operated by the Great Northern and the Duluth, Missabe and Iron Range Railroads. *Charles R. Wickman*

When the C&NW began handling iron ore pellets from the Menominee and Marquette Iron Ranges, they added extensions on the fleet. When the extensions and other rebuilding work was done, the ore cars had the letter "R" added to the right of the car number. *Patrick C. Dorin*

Burlington Northern 99778 is a 100-ton capacity ore car, which is 35 feet long. This type of car did not operate on the conventional ore docks, but rather went through a car dumper for unloading taconite pellets at the Superior, Wisconsin, ore docks. *Patrick C. Dorin*

This photo illustrates the new BNSF reporting marks for the merger Burlington Northern Santa Fe. BNSF number 600319 has the original merged company's insignia—the circle with Burlington Northern Santa Fe lettering. *Patrick C. Dorin*

The C&NW constructed a fleet of larger ore cars with 100-ton capacity for handling all-rail ore from the Menominee and Marquette Ranges and for the ore movement from the central Wisconsin mines for the steel industry in the Chicago area and elsewhere where it was needed. *Patrick C. Dorin*

# Chapter 6
# GONDOLAS

There are several types of gondolas in operation on the North American railroads. The two basic types include open top cars and covered cars with a removable cover. Depending upon the type of car and the freight for which it is designed for, there are flat bottom gondolas as well as equipment with hopper doors.

Gondolas are designed as short as 40 feet and as long as over 75 feet. The height of the cars varies again as to the type of freight for which it is intended. There are both low side and high side gondolas. Some cars are equipped with high ends for handling such traffic as logs and other material. The high ends provide protection for keeping logs and other types of freight from going over the ends.

Commodities that are immune to rain or snow can be handled in the open top, flat bottom equipment. Commodities that can be weather sensitive would need to be handled in covered gondolas for protection. One example of a commodity handled in open top gondolas in northern Indiana was sand. The sand would be loaded into the cars with front end loaders.

At the destination, the sand was unloaded by bucket cranes. Iron ore has been a commodity handled in flat bottom gondolas when there has been a shortage of hopper cars. It would be unloaded in the same manner as sand or gravel.

It is interesting to note that because of the heavier weight of sand, rock and iron ores, these commodities are loaded in a heap at each end of the car over the trucks.

As mentioned above, there are types of gondolas with hopper doors. The types of freight handled by such equipment can include various types of rock material, sand, and even such traffic as wood chips. Machinery is another type of freight that can be handled in gondolas.

Gondolas play an important role for freight handling, and one can often observe several gondolas in the consist of all types of freight trains. There have even been situations where gondolas are operated in unit trains for transporting sand, rock and other commodities.

Chicago and North Western 40-foot gondola, number 260637, is loaded with what appears to be scrap wooden ties at Superior in April 1994. The car was painted black with white lettering and carries the CNW reporting marks and the company insignia. This type of gondola was very common during the 1940s through the 1970s. *Dan Mackey*

This Milwaukee Road 50-foot gondola is equipped with bulkheads for handling pulpwood logs for the paper industry. The entire number is not visible in this photo. The car is part of the 92110 series. *Dan Mackey*

Wisconsin Central gondola is part of the 55000 series and was in general service when photographed in the 1980s.

WC 50-foot gondola number 55043 is loaded with scrap wood. This was in a group of cars painted white with red lettering. *Dan Mackey*

When the Canadian Pacific acquired the Soo Line (although previously it did have controlling interest in the company stock), the cars were painted with the CP Rail and sub-lettered for the Soo. Note the SOO reporting marks for this gondola, number 63392. *Dan Mackey*

Rail Gon, which was a Nationwide Gondola Pool, painted the equipment black with yellow trim. In this case, the car carries the Denver and Rio Grande Western reporting marks. The car is 50 feet long with an approximate 100-ton capacity. *Dan Mackey*

Originally a Soo Line gondola with bulkheads, the car was sold to the Wisconsin Central when the new company was created. The Soo reporting marks have been replaced with the letters "WC." *Dan Mackey*

The Gateway Western Railroad is a regional rail carrier, and painted equipment black with gold lettering and white reporting marks. GWWR 3070 has a capacity of 100 tons. *Dan Mackey*

Kansas City Southern gondola number 800229 is in the 50-foot category and the capacity of the car is close to 100 tons. *Dan Mackey*

WC 66221 is shown here with its white color scheme, red lettering with black reporting marks, number, and data. *Dan Mackey*

BNSF gondola number 505000 has interesting corrugated panels on each side of the car. The car's capacity is just over 80 tons with a length in the 50-feet category. *Dan Mackey*

Low side Northern Pacific gondola number 56035 (56025–56049) has a 65-foot, 6-inch inside length with an outside length of 70 feet, 8 inches. This group of gondolas have end doors to accommodate different types of loading. The car was painted black with white lettering, numbers and data. *Dan Mackey*

The Algoma Central owned and operated a fleet of bulkhead gondolas, 1001–1400 series, for handling 8-foot long pulpwood logs. The cars were 66 feet, 8 inches outside length. The photo illustrates how the pulpwood logs could be loaded in this type of car. The reporting marks AC, and the car number, were painted at the far left ends of each side of the car. *Dan Mackey*

The Wisconsin Central also owned and operated gondolas for handling pulpwood logs in northern Wisconsin and Michigan. WC 65053 is equipped with end posts designed to brace the logs at the end of the car. *Dan Mackey*

# Chapter 7
# FLAT CARS

A flat car is just exactly what the word is—a car with only a flat deck for loading many types of weather immune freight. This would include various types of machinery, farm tractors, rail, and the list can go on. There are a number of flat car designs with a bulkhead at each end of the car. The purpose of this design is to safe guard equipment from rolling off the end of the car. The cars are known as "bulkhead flats," and are often used for handling pulpwood en route to paper mills, and many other types of commodities.

Flat cars range in length from 40 feet to over 75 feet, depending upon the type of freight traffic the equipment is designed for. As with all types of freight, regardless of the type of car (except for bulk commodities in hopper cars or gondolas), the shipment must be tied down appropriately to the flat bed for safety of the equipment as well as for the safety of people and other equipment next to the railroad track.

It should be noted that flat cars are not to be confused with intermodal cars, even though intermodal is basically built as a flat car. Intermodal cars are covered later in this book.

Burlington Northern flat car number 606770 is part of the 606723 to 606772 series. The car is 56 feet, 9 inches long and has a load capacity of just over 88 tons. *Dan Mackey*

Southern Railway flat car number 150674 illustrates the frame work of the equipment below the floor. This particular car was constructed with a wood floor, part of which has been lost. However, with this type of floor, it is relatively easy to repair. Car number 150674 appears to be in the 50-foot category with a capacity of 77 tons. The car was no longer on the Norfolk Southern roster moving into the 21st Century. *Dan Mackey*

Here is an example of how heavy and high/wide loads can be handled on flat cars. Southern number 150674 is part of a group coupled together to handle this high/wide storage tank which takes up at least three flat cars. Note how the end of the load extends over the 150674. *Dan Mackey*

This photo illustrates the complete load, part of 150674, which is being handled by much longer flat in the middle with the other end extending over another flat similar to the 150674. *Dan Mackey*

Burlington Northern number 617038 is a bulkhead flat car in the 50-foot category. Bulkheads are a very safe way to handle various types of commodities by keeping the load secure within the car. Thus, the load is kept from sliding on the car in either direction due to the slack action of the freight train. *Dan Mackey*

British Columbia bulkhead flat car number 817456 is in the 50-foot category and painted black with white lettering, numbers and data. *Dan Mackey*

Former Great Northern bulkhead flat car number X4729 finished its career after revenue freight service as a work car. The bulkheads are quite a bit different from the other bulkhead flat cars illustrated in this chapter. *Dan Mackey*

Burlington Northern bulkhead flat car number 62002 is part of the freight train rolling by the UNIVERSITY station sign near Minneapolis. There are a variety of bulkheads, as one can observe to the right of the 62002. *Dan Mackey*

Flat cars can be designed to handle many types of specific commodities or specialty loads. For example, this flat car has the structure designed to handle railroad wheels. *Dan Mackey*

Flat cars can handle just about any type of freight. The example shown here is how a flat car is handling three new delivery trucks en route to its destination. *Dan Mackey*

Soo Line flat car number 5409 is handling a load of railroad ties. The ties are tied to the floor of the car. Much of the car itself is hidden by the weeds alongside the track. *Dan Mackey*

Burlington Northern flat car number 610221 is handling a railroad Maintenance of Way vehicle, which is equipped with railroad wheels as well as roadway tires. The vehicle is tied down at both ends to the flat car to ensure safe handling. *Dan Mackey*

This Burlington Northern bulkhead flat number 617677 is handling a load of steel. The car was painted in the Cascade Green with White lettering and numbers. The bulkheads provide excellent protection keeping loads from sliding. *Dan Mackey*

Santa Fe's heavy-duty flat car, number 90020, is equipped with four trucks for handling loads of well over 100 tons. *Dan Mackey*

JTTX number 930551 (from Trailer Train Leasing) is a bulkhead flat with additional bracing for handling and securing loads such as lumber. The car is approximately 85 feet long. *Dan Mackey*

Flat car HTTX 93187 is another leased car from Trailer Train. *Dan Mackey*

Another example of trucks being shipped through the use of the 85-foot Trailer Train flat cars generally used for handling truck trailers. *Dan Mackey*

CP 316600 is another example of a bulkhead flat designed to handle shipments that could be weather damaged through the use of a special covering. *Dan Mackey*

It can also be said that flat cars can carry anything. Well, in this case, it is true as OTTX 97228 is handling a damaged bulkhead flat car without its trucks. *Dan Mackey*

This is an old photo from the Duluth, South Shore and Atlantic Railway when their new ore dock and approach was being constructed in Marquette, Michigan, in October 1931. A group of DSS&A flat cars, in the 40-foot category, are coupled together for handling the steel beams for the approach trestle. *DSS&A Photo, Soo Line Historical Society*

The Duluth, Winnipeg & Pacific is owned by the Canadian National. The "Peg's" (The company nickname) reporting marks were DWC. This bulkhead flat car (number 605783) was painted black with white lettering and green bulkheads. The car was photographed at Superior in May 1992. *Bob Blomquist*

The tri-level cars were designed for transporting new automobiles. Canadian Pacific number 556549 was painted in the attractive Canadian Pacific red colors, but unfortunately was targeted for graffiti. The cars were once designated tri-level flat cars. CP Rail is no longer an insignia for the Canadian Pacific, which has now reverted back to its full name instead of simply CP Rail. *Bob Blomquist*

# Chapter 8
# TANK CARS

Tank cars are designed for handling liquid commodities, which can include slurries. As with most other freight equipment, there are a variety of tank cars in service in North America. Among the most prominent of commodities handled by tank cars are the petroleum products. Other types of commodities include chemicals and agricultural products.

Tank cars are generally designed with a circular body. The liquid commodities are loaded through the top of the car, and unloaded through a valve at one end or at the bottom of the car depending upon the design.

As a side bar note, there have been tank cars designed for unit train service that have a connecting hose between the cars. This was designed for loading or unloading cars without having to switch the individual cars for the loading.

Tank cars range in size from as short as in the 30-foot category to over 50 feet long. Again it depends upon the type of commodity the car is designed to handle.

Most of the tank cars in service in North America are owned by private companies. Many of the individual railroads have owned tank cars for freight service or company service transporting fuel for the locomotive fleet.

The following photos illustrate the types of tank cars that are or have been in operation in North America.

The private car line TILX's tank car number 135185 is designed to handle molten sulfur, as one can observe from the yellow spill from the top of car over the side. The car carries the words "Molten Sulfur" at the right end of the car—just to the left of further instructions and data. The capacity of this tank appears to be 148,000 pounds, although the lettering is a bit hazy. *Dan Mackey*

GATX 1258 is in the 50-foot category. This photo illustrates this type of tank car with railing along the walks on both sides of the top of the car. Note the loading areas in the middle of the top of this tank car. *Dan Mackey*

Another example of the top of a tank car illustrates the ladder system and the railings for the center of the top's loading area. The car's reporting marks and number, as one can see, is not visible. *Dan Mackey*

NATX number 16413's length is in the 30-foot category. The car is spotted at an oil refinery in Superior, Wisconsin. *Dan Mackey*

AFPX 413347 is a tank car assigned to handle molten sulphur traffic. *Dan Mackey*

AMIX 300012 is designed for handling liquid food products. The MCP insignia with corn cobs as part of the art work indicates that the car is designed for liquid corn products. *Dan Mackey*

GATX 87363 is over 50 feet long with a load capacity of just over 70 tons. *Dan Mackey*

GATX 65154, with the DBK insignia meaning Dry Branch Kaolin, was designed to handle a clay product. *Dan Mackey*

NATX 17030 has a capacity of over 90 tons and was designed for handling corn products. Note the corn cob insignia to the right side of the center ladder. *Dan Mackey*

AMIX 200021, in the 30-foot category, was also designed for handling corn products. *Dan Mackey*

ACFX 82042 has a loading capacity of 98 tons. *Dan Mackey*

TILX 251817 is over 50 feet long and has a capacity of over 100 tons. Note the yellow safety stripes on the side of the car, which is an excellent way of warning motorists that a train is rolling over the road or street crossing during the night. *Dan Mackey*

UTLX 25621 is leased by Engelhard for handling the company's liquid or gas products. *Dan Mackey*

Union Tank Car Company UTLX 78567 is a rather interesting tank car. The short car is less than 30 feet long and has a capacity of just over 85 tons. *Dan Mackey*

ACFX 84355 is shown here at an oil refinery in Superior, Wisconsin. The car will be taking a load of a Petroleum product. *Dan Mackey*

MCP (corn products) SYRX 200074 has a load limit of 100 tons. *Dan Mackey*

This is an Archers Daniel Midland tank number 43119 with the reporting marks ADMX. The car has a capacity in the area of 100 tons. *Dan Mackey*

Although many, if not most, tank cars are owned by private companies, a number of the railroads did own their own tank cars for various types of commodities. This tank car was owned by the Chicago Great Western, with the reporting marks CGW, and the car number is 287. The photo of the car was taken in September 1988. *Bob Blomquist*

CGTX 14372 has a load limit of 201,700 pounds. The car is designed to handle a commodity know as caustic soda. *Dan Mackey*

TILX 251817 has a load limit of 211,400 pounds. Note the yellow stripes on the side of the car for crossing protection at night. The yellow stripes will show up brightly in the headlights of an automobile approaching a crossing with a train rolling by. *Patrick C. Dorin*

GATX 45437 has an interesting commodity listed in red letters— "Steep Water." The author is not sure just exactly what that means. *Dan Mackey*

MNCX number 1018 has a capacity of 100 tons and is designed for handling corn syrup. The car is owned by a company that produced corn products. *Dan Mackey*

ADMX number 43091 is designed for handling carbon dioxide. The tank car has an attractive color scheme including the Archer Daniels Midland insignia. *Dan Mackey*

ACFX 71927 is in service for the Engelhard Company. The car has a load limit of just over 100 tons. *Bob Blomquist*

This Union Tank Car Company car, UTLX number 78567, is a shorter version of the tank car types in operation in North America. This particular car is less than 30 feet long. *Dan Mackey*

GATX 39900 has three loading entries on top of the car. Note the railings on top of the car, which are there for the safety of employees when getting the car ready for loading. *Dan Mackey*

TEIX 255 is operated by Van Gas, as one can observe from the insignia at the center of the car side. The car is designed for handling liquefied petroleum gas. It is somewhat difficult to determine the load limit, but it appears to be just over 75 tons. *Dan Mackey*

ACFX 71113 brings up the rear of a freight train on the BNSF on the south side of St. Paul, Minnesota. *Dan Mackey*

ARIX 1262 is designed to handle carbon dioxide as a refrigerated liquid. Note the catwalk on top of the tank car along with the railings for safety. *Dan Mackey*

Union Tank Car Company, UTLX number 58620, is part of a thru freight train heading south out of Superior, Wisconsin, on the Wisconsin Central in May 1993. Note the carload of pulpwood behind the tank car, which is headed for the paper mills in Central Wisconsin. *Dan Mackey*

Here is an example of two tank cars spotted at an industrial siding. Although the cars are loaded through the top of the car, they can be unloaded easily through the bottom of the tank. The car to the left of the pair is GATX 82948. *Dan Mackey*

Union Tank Car Company tank car (UTLX) number 57834 has a capacity of 101 tons, or 202,000 pounds. The car is part of the consist of a Wisconsin Central train south of Superior, Wisconsin. *May 1993, Dan Mackey*

CGTX number 14372 has lettering to the right that the car is designed to handle caustic soda. The car has a load limit of 201,700 pounds. *June 1993, Dan Mackey*

UTLX 47477 is a larger tank car over 50 feet long with a capacity of 192,000 pounds. *Feb. 1994, Dan Mackey*

# Chapter 9
# INTERMODAL CARS

Intermodal cars are specifically designed flat cars for handling semi-trailers and/or containers. The cars range in length from the 50- or 55-foot category to 85 feet plus. The shorter cars can handle one semi-trailer, as long as 53 feet, while the longer cars are designed for two trailers. The 85-foot cars can handle two 40-foot trailers. However, the 40-foot trailers are being replaced by the longer 53-foot design. Many of the 53-foot trailers are handled on a flat in the 55-foot category.

Intermodal cars were first designed—back as far as the late 1920s—for handling the shorter trailers from that era, which were as short as 20 feet. As time went on, the cars were lengthened to handle the longer trailers.

Eventually, new designs began to be developed, such as the Flexi-van which came about in full service on the New York Central. The Flexi-van cars were designed to handle the semi-trailer without its wheels. They were designed in such a way that a truck driver could back the trailer to the flat car, and have the container slide off on to a turn-table receiving unit. Once the container was attached to the receiving unit, it could be turned to have the trailer totally on the car.

The New York Central design was well received, and at one time, the Central operated basically an overnight truck service between Chicago and New York with the Flexi-van containers on board. The Flexi-van design was also used for handling mail and express traffic not only on the New York Central, but also the Illinois Central and the Milwaukee Road. The Milwaukee Road's Fast Mail train (overnight between Chicago and the Twin Cities) operated with Flexi-van equipment as part of the consist.

The following photos illustrate the various types of intermodal cars (and trailers and containers) operated on the North American railroads.

The intermodal transport of semi-trailers and containers on intermodal cars combines the economical benefits of truck and rail transport. A short line in northern Minnesota, known as the Minnesota, Dakota and Western (note the MDW insignia on the trailer) handles trailers on flat cars for movement to the CN and the BNSF railroads. The MDW owns their own trailers for paper loading, which are placed on intermodal flats for movement over the rail lines. The reporting marks TTX stands for the Trailer Train Company. This type of car can handle two 40-foot trailers, but only one when 53-foot trailers are loaded on board. *Dan Mackey*

Trailer Train intermodal car number 912620 is shown here in northern Minnesota en route to an intermodal terminal for handling trailers loaded with paper for a wide variety of destinations throughout the Midwest and well beyond for that matter. *Dan Mackey*

This end view of an intermodal flat and trailer illustrates the mechanism for securing the trailer to the rail car for safe and secure transportation. *Dan Mackey*

# *Chapter 10*
# AUTO RACKS

Auto racks are a rather unique type of equipment designed for handling automobiles and various types of smaller trucks, such as pick-up trucks. Automobiles are often shipped from the manufacturer's plants in tri-level cars, while smaller trucks are handled with bi-level cars.

Vehicles are loaded with ramps that can be elevated or lowered to accommodate the different levels. The auto racks are completely enclosed for the protection of the new vehicles.

The rack cars are in the 85-foot category and can handle up to 15 automobiles depending upon the size of the autos. A tri-level rack can handle 12 automobiles of standard size, or up 15 vehicles of the smaller size and length.

Bi-level rack cars are generally designed to handle various types of trucks. The capacity can vary depending upon the length of the vehicles.

The following photo illustrates a tri-level car.

Trailer Train, TTGX number 913416, a Soo Line tri-level car designed for handling new automobiles from the auto manufacturing plant to distribution terminals. At that point, the automobiles are unloaded and reloaded on to highway auto carriers for transportation to car dealers. These auto carriers provide an economical mode of transport over rail lines, with a high degree of safety. Since the new autos are in enclosed cars, they have weather protection as well as safety from other hazards. Although barely visible, the tri-level car to the right of the Soo equipment is a Southern Pacific Railroad car. The cars are part of a consist of a Soo Line train on the former Milwaukee Road just southeast of St. Paul, Minnesota. *Dan Mackey*

# Chapter 11
# CABOOSES

Cabooses were in operation on the North American railroads since the mid-1800s until the early 1990s. The primary purpose of the caboose was for a crew to ride the rear of a freight train. The crew's work included watching the freight cars ahead, especially going around curves, to make sure nothing was going wrong. For example, the trucks were specifically observed to make sure that none of the journal boxes (where the wheel axles fit into the side frames) were burning up. If they were (and steel can catch on fire), it meant that the journal box was known as a "hot box" and the car needed to be taken out of the train consist at the closest possible siding. If a hot box was observed the train would need to come to stop and have it inspected to determine if it could make it to the next siding. If so, the train would move slowly to the next siding and switch out the car.

A car inspector would be called to take a look at the situation, and see what could be done to take care of the problem, such as providing the appropriate lubrication in the journal. Hot boxes come about because of a lack of lubrication. Rolling bearing journals has reduced the number of hot boxes substantially.

Cabooses have been literally replaced by a computer system, known as a rear end device, and are attached to the coupler of the last car in the train.

The rear end device can provide information about the rear end of the train, such as the amount of air in the air brake system. The crew in the cab of the locomotive can secure information about the air brake system from the rear end with this relatively new computer system.

Cabooses are still in use for certain situations, such as extensive back-up moves where a crew member will ride the caboose and inform the engineer of conditions on the track and over roadways. One will find some cabooses at railroad yards, where they may be used for backup moves or other situations requiring a crew member on the rear of the train.

## BAY-WINDOW CABOOSES

We have two chapters devoted to cabooses. The first chapter covers the various types of bay-window cabooses. Part of the idea for the bay window was to provide the rear end crew with a better chance to observe the side of the train by eliminating the need to extend their head out of the car. Bay-window cabooses became quite popular with the railroad companies with the viewing advantage.

The following photos illustrate the different types of bay-window cabooses in operation throughout North America.

The Green Bay and Western, known as the Green Bay Route (note the lettering below the bay window), had an attractive yellow scheme for its cabooses. The GBW number 617 is on the rear of a freight train that operated between Green Bay and Winona, Minnesota. The GB&W actually extended east of Green Bay to Kewaunee on, Lake Michigan, where the company connected with a rail ferry that sailed across the lake to Ludington, Michigan. The company symbol was outlined in white with a red background and white letters: Green Bay Route. *Bob Blomquist*

Duluth, Missabe and Iron Range Railway caboose number C-191 could be described as a mini-bay window. There was seating next to the window so that crew could observe the condition and safe movements of the train. With the smaller bay window, the crew would have to lean their head into the window area to see ahead. The C-191 was originally built with a cupola, but was rebuilt when the car went into service at the new Thunder Bird mine, where the ore train operated through the loading system. A cupola caboose would not have cleared the loading area. *Bob Blomquist*

DM&IR caboose number C-209 was another caboose modified for operation through the loading areas at one of the taconite pellet plants on the Missabe Iron Range. This steel caboose lost its cupola for the modification. *Bob Blomquist*

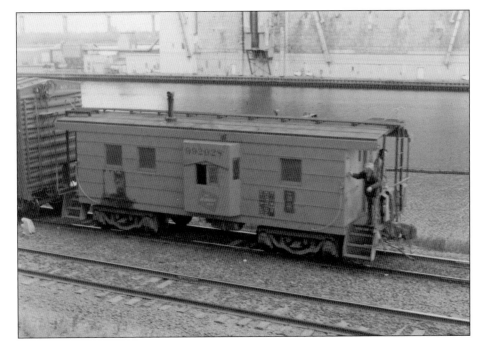

The Milwaukee Road owned and operated a fleet of bay-window cabooses with rib sides. The cars were painted in the company's orange color scheme. This car, number 992098, was photographed on the rear of the Duluth–St. Paul time freight, which operated daily with trackage rights over the former Northern Pacific line between the Twin Cities and the Twin Ports. *Bob Blomquist*

Another example of a Milwaukee Road bay-window, rib side caboose was number 991939, in the orange color scheme with yellow ends. *Bob Blomquist*

Milwaukee Road number 992217 was part of the later caboose fleet with smooth sides. *Bob Blomquist*

The Chicago and North Western once had a fleet of wood cupola cabooses, but opted for the bay-window variety when they began modernizing the group. Car number 10983 was painted in the original yellow color that the company adopted for the motive power and passenger equipment. The insignia on this car was the "Employee Owned" symbol. *Bob Blomquist*

This photo shows the opposite side of C&NW bay-window caboose number 10983, which carried the original company yellow scheme with the Employee Owned insignia. *Bob Blomquist*

As time went on, windows were blocked out, such as the 10924 shown here. The company modified the placement of the insignia, with an American flag at the other end of the car. This car's portrait was taken in March 1982. *Bob Blomquist*

For a while, when the company was employee owned, the words, "We're Employee Owned" were part of the lettering as can be observed at the lower left end. Caboose number 11194 has had its windows blocked out, and has the company insignia at both ends. *1979, Bob Blomquist*

This 1982 photo illustrates the insignia at the left end, and the American flag at the right end. The C&NW's yellow cabooses also had a green roof as can be observed with car number 11121. *Bob Blomquist*

C&NW bay-window caboose number 10378 had the Employee Owned insignias at both ends without any additional colors as one could observe on several other cars about the same time as this photo in 1978. C&NW yellow cabooses also had silver paint on the stack. *Bob Blomquist*

C&NW's bay-window number 11145 also had the Employee Owned insignia, which because of the lack of color were sometimes difficult to see. This car was photographed on the rear of a freight train at the Itasca yard which is at the far east end of Superior. *1978, Bob Blomquist*

Here is an example of the roof of a C&NW bay-window caboose. Note the green colors and the red markers at this end of the car. *Bob Blomquist*

Milwaukee Road bay-window number 992217 was one in the final groups of cabooses. This car is on the rear of the overnight Milwaukee Road freight between Duluth and the St. Paul yard. The building in the background is the Duluth Union Station, which once handled passenger trains for the Great Northern and the Northern Pacific. The depot is now sited as a historical building and serves as the headquarters of the North Shore Scenic Railroad. The NSSR operates passenger excursions between Duluth and Two Harbors on a daily basis during the summers. *1982, Bob Blomquist*

Part of the Missouri Pacific bay-window caboose fleet had longer end platforms. Car number 13735 was painted blue with the company's "Eagle" insignia with the red circle for the background. This was part of the last cabooses purchased by the MP. *Patrick C. Dorin*

Although this caboose does not have a bay window or a cupola, it is an example of cabooses that were often used for yard transfer services. The cars played a major role for backup moves where the switchman or yard foreman could ride on the platform with end railings. This former Great Northern caboose has had its "X-927" number replaced with the BN sub-lettering and the new number 10927. Although the wording at the bottom of the car is somewhat hard to read, it says, "What's your safe score today?" To the far left of the car there is very small wording, "Yard Service Only." *Superior, May 1974, Bob Blomquist*

Western Pacific bay-window caboose number 441 has safety stripes on the bay window for the safety of crews close to the track. The car was painted with an attractive red color with a silver roof, and black exhaust stacks on the roof. This car was a run-thru car all the way to the Chicago and North Western, and is shown here at Superior, Wisconsin, in the late 1980s. *Bob Blomquist*

The Great Northern Railway had only a small fleet of bay-window cabooses, which were operated on the taconite trains (note the ore cars). GN number X 184's roof level is somewhat lower than the taconite cars. Note the fresh painting of the rebuilt GN cars with the extensions to handle the lighter per cubic-foot of the taconite pellets. The taconite trains ran from the Allouez ore yard in Superior to one of the taconite plants. The empty train went through the loader, and when loaded the train returned directly to Superior. The taconite cars were not unloaded on the ore docks, but rather through a car dumper. The pellets were stockpiled and were transported to the ore dock by a conveyor belt system for the boat loading. *Bob Blomquist*

# Chapter 12
# CUPOLA CABOOSES

The cupola caboose was a car designed with an upper level viewing area, which was located above the roof of the car. In a sense it was like a box with seating at the upper level to provide the viewing necessary to observe the freight train as it rolled along.

Since the cupola was on top of the car, the caboose had a modified ladder/step system for the crews to get into the seating. The seating faced both directions, which provided a convenient way to observe the train movements either way. The cupola had seating on both sides of the car. Thus there were four seats in the cupola. The two on each side faced each other.

By having seating on both sides of the cupola, it was relatively easy for two crew members to sit on each side of the car to observe the train. This provided an opportunity for the ability to spot a "hot box" (a truck journal either smoking or literally on fire) before an accident or even a major derailment took place.

The following photos illustrate some of the various types of cupola cabooses in operation on the railroad system.

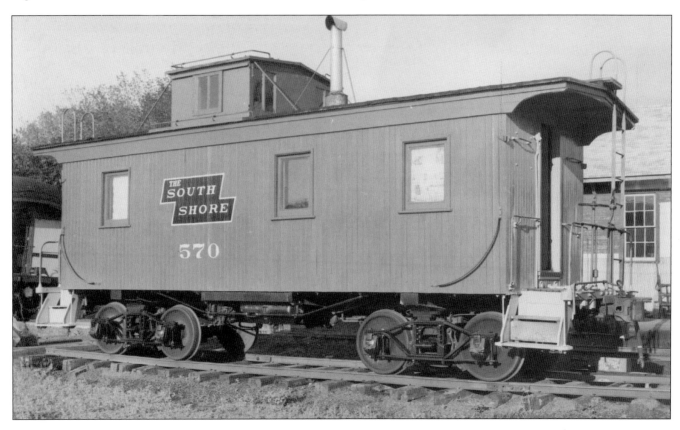

This Duluth, South Shore and Atlantic Railroad caboose, number 570, is an excellent example of the wood cabooses that saw service in North America for well over 150 years. The car is in the 35-feet length category and has 3 windows on each side. The car was painted box car red with black insignia with white lettering. Note the older style of the trucks, which are known as Arch-Bar trucks. The DSS&A operated thru-trains between Superior, Wisconsin, and Saulte Ste. Marie and St. Ignace, Michigan. For many years, crews often had cabooses directly assigned to them, and consequently cabooses would be changed at crew change points. *Harold K. Vollrath*

This Duluth, Winnipeg and Pacific Railway caboose, number 76923, served on DW&P freight trains between Duluth and Ranier, Minnesota, as well as over the border to Fort Francis, Ontario. This photo was taken at the Peg's West Duluth yard, which no longer exists as the terminal was moved over to a point southwest of Superior, known as Pokegama. Note the handrails and ladders are painted white for additional safety levels. *Patrick C. Dorin*

This Duluth, Missabe & Iron Range Railway caboose, number C-9, included a door on the side of the car for loads less than carload freight and other material including company mail. This caboose was part of the C-8 to C-10 series and today is on display at the Lake Superior Railroad Museum in Duluth, Minnesota. The Chicago and North Western Bi-level commuter coach to the right is also part of a three-car group operated for excursions on the North Shore Scenic Railroad between Duluth and Two Harbors, Minnesota. The NSSR line was once part of the Duluth, Missabe & Iron Range Railway. *Patrick C. Dorin*

The Elgin, Joliet and Eastern Railroad had the company slogan within the insignia as illustrated with this caboose, number 504. The phrase "Chicago Outer Belt" was very appropriate for the company as the route extended southwest from Waukegan, Illinois, and then directly south to Joliet. Continuing eastward, the route split at Griffith, Indiana, with one line going north to Gary and the other east to Porter. The caboose was painted in the orange colors of the EJ&E. Number 504 is shown here at Waukegan in October 1966. *Harold K. Vollrath Collection*

The Duluth, Winnipeg and Pacific came up with a neat insignia that replaced the former Maple Leaf symbol. This caboose was painted in the Grand Trunk blue with white lettering. The DWP included the words "Delivered With Pride" on the bottom line leading to the "P." Caboose number 53101 is shown here at the old West Duluth, Minnesota, yard. Note the two Canadian National cabooses at both ends of the DWP car. *Patrick C. Dorin*

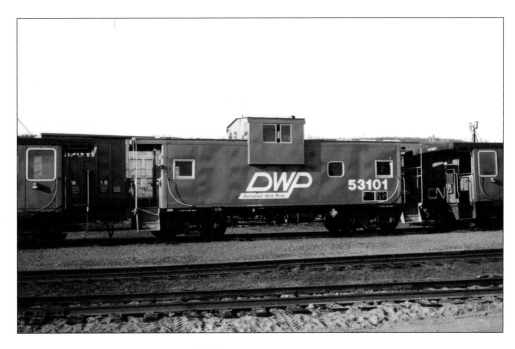

This Burlington Northern caboose number 10387 was a former Great Northern car built with a streamlined cupola, which was slanted at both ends. This car was photographed at a caboose track in the former GN Superior, Wisconsin, freight yard. The car was painted in the BN green with yellow ends for safety. *1979, Bob Blomquist*

BN caboose number 10382 illustrates the opposite side of the BN number 10387 illustrated previously. *Superior, 1987, Bob Blomquist*

This Burlington Route caboose, number 13522, became BN number 11467. Note the original reporting marks CB&Q above the original car number. Barely visible at the right end of the car below the BN car number are the initials "BN." The car was painted in a silver scheme and originally had 4 windows on this side of the car, but the one closest to cupola was blanked out. Note the radio antenna at this end of the caboose on the roof. The car was still in operation in Superior in 1980. *Bob Blomquist*

This Burlington Route caboose has had its original number and reporting marks painted out, and replaced by the new BN number 11457 at the right end with the letters BN barely visible below the new number. *Bob Blomquist*

Duluth, Missabe & Iron Range Railway wood caboose number C-492 went through a rebuilding process and was painted in what could be called a golden yellow color with a maroon lettering as well as numbers. The roof was also painted maroon. The car sides were rebuilt with wood panels. Notice how even the window frames were done in the very attractive maroon. The caboose has the marker lights at the left end indicating that the car is part of a train. *Bob Blomquist*

DM&IR caboose number C-215 was part of the early order of extended vision cupola cabooses. The company's insignia is getting weathered and the right side of it is disappearing. *Bob Blomquist*

Northern Pacific caboose, now renumbered 10426 with BN reporting marks, is one of the typical cabooses owned and operated by the NP. The car's portrait was taken in March 1978 when the BN merger was eight years old, thus the reason for the BN reporting marks. *Bob Blomquist*

The last paint scheme for the Great Northern cabooses was blue. The wide vision cupola ex-GN caboose in this photo still carries the final blue colors but with the new BN 10079 lettering and number. The car also carries the final GN "goat" insignia with the lettering "Great Northern" outside the circle. *Feb. 1978, Bob Blomquist*

Great Northern wooden caboose, in this photo as BN 11220, still retains its GN scheme in 1977, well into the BN merger. One outstanding characteristic about GN cabooses was the wide variety of the wording for safety at the center-bottom of the side. The message for this renumbered car was "Make Your Way The Safe Way." There were a number of GN cabooses that were constructed of steel of this same design. All GN cabooses carried the wording "Radio Equipped." *Sept., 1977, Bob Blomquist*

This GN caboose, now numbered BN 10986, was a shorter version of the cars with four windows on each side. This car did not have the lettering "Radio Equipped," but did have the safety message, "Be Wise, Beware, Be Safe." *Nov. 1980, Bob Blomquist*

This Burlington bright silver painted caboose carries the company insignia. The car number is 157, and is shown here on the side of the wide vision cupola. Number 157 is actually owned by the Fort Worth and Denver, a subsidiary of the Burlington Route, also known as the Chicago, Burlington and Quincy with the CB&Q reporting marks. The FW&D lettering is painted black, and is very small lettering just above the window at the left end on this side of the car. *1982, Bob Blomquist*

Still another wide vision cupola caboose for the Burlington Route was this Colorado and Southern number 10635, with C&S initials above the window at the left end of the car. *1978, Bob Blomquist*

This Burlington Northern caboose, BN 10113, still carries the Burlington Route insignia and silver colors in this 1978 portrait. *Bob Blomquist*

It has been 10 years since the BN merger, and the Burlington caboose number 10628 is actually a Colorado and Southern car, a subsidiary of the "Q" and now the BN, but does not have any BN reporting marks. The 10628 is a good example of the Burlington Route's color scheme on the cabooses. *1980, Bob Blomquist*

GN steel caboose minus its original X- number, now with its BN number 11386, illustrates the attractive red color scheme (although weathered a bit by 1980), and the reminder lettering applied to all cabooses. For this car, "Think Safety Work Safely" was the message. All Great Northern cabooses carried some type of a safety message, which were there to remind folks to always be safe. The messages on the cabooses must have worked well because there were fewer accidents. Many GN employees told this writer that it was one of the best companies to work for. I had the same experience while working on the GN for a couple of summers during my college years. *1980, Bob Blomquist*

This wide vision cupola caboose received the blue colors prior to the BN merger in 1970. The car still carried the blue colors and the most recent lettering and insignia when its portrait was taken in Superior during the summer of 1978. The new BN number was 10079. *Bob Blomquist*

This ex-Northern Pacific, now BN number 10039 in this 1979 photo, received the NP's last color scheme applications to the caboose fleet of green with yellow applied to one end. *Superior, 1979, Bob Blomquist*

Eight years into the BN merger, this NP caboose does have its BN number of 10036. Note the wide vision cupola and the four windows on this side of the car. *1978, Bob Blomquist*

Ex-NP caboose, now BN 10032, illustrates the yellow application at the right end of the car in this photo. It should be noted that the NP cabooses with the green scheme had yellow ends. *Superior, 1978, Bob Blomquist*

When the Burlington Northern merger was in full swing, many cabooses were repainted in a green with yellow ends for safety. BN caboose number 11392 is a former Great Northern caboose in the attractive scheme applied by the new company. *1978, Bob Blomquist*

Burlington Northern wide vision caboose number 12356 has no side windows, except for those in the cupola. There is no doubt that the yellow ends of the BN cabooses greatly improved visibility for safety reasons. *1980, Bob Blomquist*

BN caboose number 10225 illustrates the placement of the three windows on this side. Note the silver paint on the stack. *1977, Bob Blomquist*

BN number 10034 shows the placement of the four windows on the opposite side. *1977, Bob Blomquist*

BN number 12175 has a slightly different type of window on this side of the car. Notice the somewhat smaller window just to the left of the stack. *1978, Bob Blomquist*

BN caboose number 10295 has four windows on this side of the car. *1978, Bob Blomquist*

Conrail caboose number 23112 had circular windows and slightly slanted cupola. The car was painted in Conrail blue color scheme with white lettering and numbers. *1980, Bob Blomquis*

Still another version of a Conrail caboose, number 13339, with rectangular windows. *1980, Bob Blomquist*

Conrail caboose number 22653 is a rather unusual rebuild. The cupola windows have been blocked out and the car has been partially rebuilt with a bay window. The window at the right end of the car has been blocked out as well. Notice how part of the Conrail insignia has been blocked out with the installation of the bay window. The car had not been repainted as of August 1980 when this photo was taken. *Bob Blomquist*

For quite a few years since the 1960s, cabooses often remained with run-thru trains from one railroad to another. This Union Pacific caboose number 25205 was photographed at Superior on the Burlington Northern's track in the late 1970s. *Bob Blomquist*

Chicago and North Western's wide vision cupola caboose number 12561 has had the windows in the cupola blocked out. However, the car has one window at the left end of this side of the car. The car had been repainted as well with the words, "Since 1848 Pulling Together." The C&NW insignia still had the words "Chicago" at the top and "System" at the bottom. In addition to the lettering, many C&NW cabooses also had the American Flag as part of its décor. It does not appear that there were any additional windows on this side of the car. This photo was taken at the C&NW's caboose track at the Itasca yard in Superior, Wisconsin. *Bob Blomquist*

The Duluth, Missabe and Iron Range Railway painted their cabooses with a golden yellow color with a maroon roof and lettering. The company numbered the cars with the prefix "C" as can be observed with the number C-143 on the "Arrowhead." It can be said that the DM&IR utilized two insignias for the company—both the circular with the full name of the company including the words "Safety First" and "Arrowhead." Note how the arrowhead with the car number is directly below the circular insignia. *Bob Blomquist*

The first wide vision cupola caboose for the DM&IR was the C-200. It is shown here on the rear of a local freight consist departing downtown Duluth for Two Harbors in April 1982. Note the wide windows on the Coach-Observation car just ahead of the caboose. The train is moving northbound on trackage that had to be removed and replaced by an expressway so people could avoid driving through downtown Duluth. *Bob Blomquist*

The DM&IR invested in additional wide-vision cupola cabooses, such as the C-227 shown here. The car is on the rear of a taconite pellet train. The DM&IR cabooses also had safety stripes on the ends. *Bob Blomquist*

This Burlington Northern caboose number 10343 had a rare design for a streamlined cupola with slanted ends. The car is shown here at the former Great Northern yard in Superior in September 1978 when cabooses were still in full use. Notice how the ladders have been virtually eliminated with the removal of the catwalks on top of cabooses. *Bob Blomquist*

The BN wide vision cupola caboose, number 10646, was a typical design for this type of a car. The car is still equipped with end ladders as well as the catwalk on top of the caboose. One can observe just a small part of the catwalk and the safety platform at this end of the car. The 10646's portrait was taken at the Superior yard in 1978. *Bob Blomquist*

When the C&NW absorbed the Chicago Great Western, their cabooses began operating to a variety of areas that had not been served by the CGW. This photo was taken in Duluth, Minnesota, in May 1974. *Bob Blomquist*

The NP also invested in extended vision cupola cabooses, such as shown here with this attractive color scheme of green with yellow ends, on car number 10036. Barely visible to the left is a caboose in the BN green. *February 1975, Bob Blomquist*

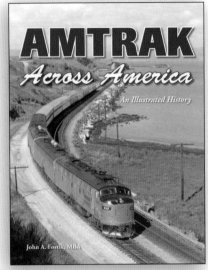
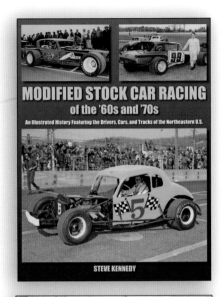
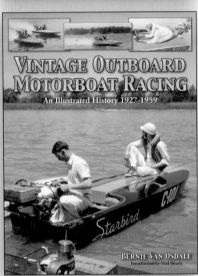
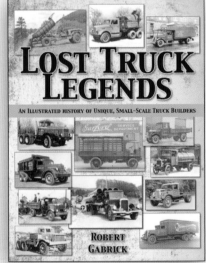
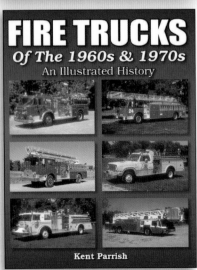
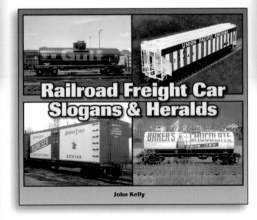
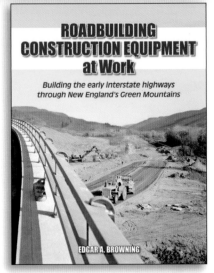